BEACH BOOK

BY KAREN DAWE

Illustrated by Joe Weissmann

A Somerville House Book
WORKMAN PUBLISHING, NEW YORK

Copyright © 1988 by
Somerville House Books
  Limited
Illustrations © 1988 by
Joe Weissmann

Produced by
Somerville House Books
  Limited
24 Dinnick Crescent
Toronto, Canada
M4N 1L5

Library of Congress
Cataloging-in-Publication
  Data
Dawe, Karen.
    The beach book and
    the beach bucket.
1. Seashore
    biology—Juvenile
    literature.
I. Weissmann, Joe.
II. Title.
QH95.7.D37 1988
574.909'46   87-40648
ISBN 0-89480-590-8 (pbk.)

Published by
Workman Publishing
708 Broadway
New York, New York 10003
Printed in the United
States of America

First printing June 1988

10 9 8 7 6 5 4 3 2 1

*For Jordan and Kelsi,
my own beach creatures,
who at an early age found
tidepools irresistible and joy
in water-filled boots.*

*Thanks to Dr. Dale Calder,
The Royal Ontario
Museum, Toronto; to
Dr. Thomas Carefoot,
Department of Zoology,
University of British
Columbia; and to my
editor, Catherine Ripley.*

Contents

If you want to know more about a beach plant or animal, turn to page 64 and find out its scientific name before you ask an expert or look in another book. The common names vary from place to place, but the scientific names are the same around the world.

You Can't Beat the Beach!

The beach is like no other place on Earth. An amazing variety of plants and animals make their home here, each with a special way of surviving in this mysterious world between land and sea. Some burrow deep into the sand; others live in tidepools or on rocks; still others are covered with seawater most of the day.

Be a beach detective. Search for clam holes in the sand. Look into tidepools and under seaweed. Listen to the beach sounds. Take your Beach Bucket along and examine some of the fascinating things that turn up.

Be a beach biologist. Ask yourself why the beach life lives the way it does. Why do those barnacles stand on their heads? How does the periwinkle skate? Why do clams clam up? You'll find some of the answers in the Beach Book.

Now, pick up your bucket and start beachcombing . . . walk the driftline, catch a crab, sort out shells. Have fun!

Beach & Bucket Tips

1 Dress for the weather. On hot summer days, wear shorts or a bathing suit and put on lots of suntan lotion. On cooler days, in spring and autumn, wear sweaters and long pants to keep warm.

2 Wear rubber boots or sneakers to protect your feet from sharp shells and pointed rocks.

3 One of the best times to go beachcombing is when the tide is on its way out. Follow the water as it uncovers the beach and see what you can find.

4 Walk around mussel beds and barnacle-covered rocks if you can. Remember—you are a giant. Your weight can crush hundreds of animals!

Beach & Bucket Tips

Watch the tide! Along some parts of the coastline, the sea comes in very fast. Remember to look up often to see where the water is—otherwise you may suddenly find yourself at sea!

5 Use the lid of your bucket as a scoop, and use the bucket to hold your discoveries. Do not crowd animals in the bucket. And most important, keep them cool—the hot sun can kill!

6 Be as gentle as possible. Many creatures are easily damaged.

7 Fill in any holes you dig. You may have covered up someone's home with your diggings.

8 Be extra careful when you turn over a rock. Many animals live attached to rocks or hide underneath them. Put the rocks back the way you found them, with the topside up, so the animals' homes are exactly the same as they were before you came along.

9 When it's time to return your discoveries to their natural surroundings, try to find the spot where you picked them up. Otherwise, put them as near as you can in a cool, protected place and cover them with a bit of seaweed.

10 Never take live animals home. They need the sea to survive.

Don't Touch!

Watch for this sign next to some of the animals in this book. Be sure not to touch anemones or other animals that have stinging cells; they can give you an itchy sting and even a blister. Be sure not to touch some of the crabs, which can give you a painful nip. And always remember not to touch fragile things like the egg cases of the moon snail—you might hurt them!

What Is a Beach?

Rock

A beach is a place that is always changing. Rain, wind and waves constantly wear at the shore, building it up and then tearing it down.

A beach is also an environment. Each day it is washed by the sea, and between the highest and lowest tides lies the part of the beach called the "intertidal area." This is the home of all the plants and animals that appear on these pages. Each one lives where it finds the amount of water, salt, light and food that it needs to survive. Some live high up where only spray from the waves reaches them; others stay mostly underwater. If you look carefully at a beach when the tide is out, you can make out broad "zones" of plants and animals that have found their special places.

And, of course, a beach is a wonderful place to have fun. But it isn't a playground to beach creatures. It is their home, and living there is a serious business.

Sand

Mud

What kind of beach are you on?

Beach Materials

• Rocks are slowly worn down by the wind and sea. Plants and animals survive on a rocky beach by clamping down tightly or moving with the waves that wash over them. You may find pebbles as small as peas and cobbles as big as basketballs; these stones were tossed against each other in the waves until very slowly they were rounded by the constant grinding. You'll discover lots of life here—clinging to, hiding under or moving over the rocks.

• The sand is actually millions and millions of tiny pieces of rock, worn from larger rocks. These pieces, or grains, are forever shifting, so creatures that dig into the sand flourish here.

• Mud is finely crushed soft rock, mixed with clay, silt, rotting plants and water. The animals that live here hide beneath the surface.

Many beaches are a mixture of these three materials, and there the life is the most varied of all.

What Is the Sea?

If you looked back at Earth from a space-craft, you would see that our planet is mostly covered by water. The water in the oceans is never still. It rises and falls in high and low tides caused by the pull of the moon and sun.

The Waves

Waves are made by the wind blowing across the surface of the sea. You can feel their power even when they are small. Stand in the surf and feel the waves gently push you as they move to shore. Then sand and pebbles are pulled from under your feet as the water rushes back to the sea. This is the same force that continually wears down rocks, changes coastlines and topples sandcastles.

Life in the Sea

Unlike the water that comes out of your faucet at home, seawater is a rich soup of dissolved mineral salts and millions of tiny animals and plants called plankton. The mineral salts (with-

out which most beach creatures could not survive) are worn from rock and washed into the sea. Most of the plankton in seawater are so small that you can't even see them. The animal plankton, called zooplankton, include the larvae, or early forms, of many of the animals in this book. The plant plankton, or phytoplankton, are the food-makers; without them, the animal life in the sea, even the zooplankton, would die.

Plants are eaten by animals, which in turn are eaten by other animals—the meat-eaters. Each is a link in a "food chain." There are hundreds of different food chains in the sea, and all of them begin with a plant.

Phytoplankton

Zooplankton

13

Discover the Driftline

The driftline is a treasure-trove of beach things. This long line of tangled seaweed, tossed-up shells and waterlogged driftwood is especially good for beachcombing after a storm, but it's always interesting because of the high tides. All sorts of drifting plants and animals come in with the tides and are left stranded on the beach when the water recedes.

BEACH PROJECT

Look along the driftline for seaweed. Rinse it in your bucket with clean seawater and rub it between your fingers. Some seaweeds will feel rough and leathery; others are slimy, which keeps them from drying out during low tide. If the seaweed is dry and crisp, put it in the water and watch it turn soft and flexible.

Find some seaweed still attached to a rock. Look at the seaweed's "holdfast," which keeps the plant tightly gripped in place. The holdfast looks like the roots of a land plant, but it doesn't supply water and minerals the way roots do; instead, it is only a big, strong anchor that keeps the seaweed secure in the pounding surf. Try swooshing the seaweed off its rock with a bucketful of water and see how successful you are!

You'll also discover small animals in the driftline, clinging to the seaweed or using it as shelter from the sun and wind. To learn about the different kinds of beach life, see the groups described on the next eight pages.

Seaweed

Seaweeds are large algae related to phytoplankton, the almost invisible algae that float in the sea. Like all plants, algae make their own food from carbon dioxide, water and sunlight. They are to the sea what grasses are to the land: the number one food producers.

You'll find seaweeds growing along shorelines in shallow water or floating offshore on the surface of the sea. Not all seaweeds are green. Biologists divide them into color groups for identification purposes. The blue-green algae are the scums on mudflats or rocks. Some of the green, brown and red types are shown on these pages.

The fronds are the seaweed's "leaves."

Rockweed

The stipe is like the stem of a land plant.

The holdfast anchors the plant to rocks.

● ROCKWEED, or bladderwrack, grows in crowded mats over rocks and tidepools. Look at the many air bladders along the fronds that help the plant float. Squeeze one between your fingers . . . pop! Now look at the swollen ends of the fronds. This is where cells are developing into new plants.

● SEA LETTUCE fronds grow in thin, ruffled sheets, sometimes three or four feet tall! Look for a bright green seaweed flattened against the rocks at low tide.

Sea Lettuce

Sugar Kelp

● SUGAR KELP is home to many sea creatures. Giant kelps grow in dense underwater forests and are a favorite food of sea urchins.

Turkish Towel

● There may be some TURKISH TOWEL in your home! Some of the red and brown seaweeds are used in everyday things such as toothpaste, paper and even ice cream. Look for the names Agar-Agar and Carrageenan on packages.

Cnidarians

Cnidarians (say "ni-dare-ee-ans") are soft, hollow animals that absorb oxygen through their skin. Some, such as jellyfish, are umbrella-shaped and swim freely; others, such as sea anemones, are tube-shaped and spend their lives attached to rocks. Both kinds of cnidarians have tentacles with stinging cells. Don't touch any cnidarians that you find: you might be hurt by their sting.

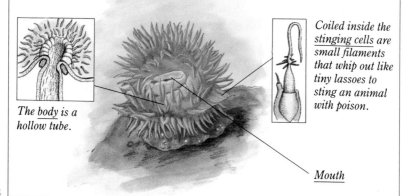

The body is a hollow tube.

Coiled inside the stinging cells are small filaments that whip out like tiny lassoes to sting an animal with poison.

Mouth

Mollusks

Mollusks are soft-bodied animals, usually covered by a shell. Some mollusks burrow; others creep or crawl; still others swim.

Each shell has growth rings just like the ones you can see inside a fallen tree. Every day the mollusk's mantle adds a tiny amount of shell to the outer edge. If you could count all of these microscopic rings, you'd know the animal's exact age!

The octopus is a shell-less mollusk. Its foot is divided into eight arms, used for crawling and catching food. Unlike clams and snails, this mollusk has a beak and can bite!

The shipworm has a shell no bigger than a fingernail, but its wormlike body can grow as long as your arm! You're not likely to see this mollusk, because it tunnels into wood with its shell and stays there for life.

Inside Mollusks

Univalves

Univalves have only one piece to their shell. Some univalves' shells are shaped in a spiral; others look like round, pointed caps. Limpets and snails, such as the whelk and moon snail, are univalves.

The gill is used for absorbing oxygen.

This mollusk touches and tastes with its tentacles.

The skinlike mantle covers the soft body, makes the shell and can be used to take in oxygen.

Most snails can see only dark and light with their eyes.

By tightly shutting its operculum, or door, the snail protects itself from other animals and from drying out.

A univalve clings to rocks, or creeps over rocks and sand, with its foot.

The radula is a tongue that is covered with rows of tiny teeth!

Bivalves

Bivalves have a two-piece shell. Many protect themselves by living deep in the sand and are connected to the outside world only by their siphons, which reach all the way up to the surface to bring in water. Inside the bivalve, gills absorb oxygen and filter food from the water.

Sometimes a grain of sand lodges between an oyster's mantle and shell. The mantle then covers it up with layers of pearly shell-building material—until one day the lowly grain of sand becomes a pearl!

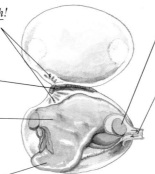

A bivalve's shell has <u>teeth</u>! They fit together and keep the two valves from slipping sideways.

The <u>hinge</u> joins the two halves, or valves.

The <u>mantle</u> covers the body, forms the siphon and makes the shell.

The bivalve moves and digs with its <u>foot</u>.

The <u>muscles</u> pull the valves closed.

The <u>siphon</u> is two tubes joined together. One tube brings in water and food; the other takes out water and waste. Sometimes the tubes are separate.

Crustaceans

Crustaceans (say "crus-tay-shuns") such as barnacles, beach hoppers and crabs are closely related to insects! They have a hard "crust," or skeleton, on the outside of their body, and the three body parts are divided into many segments—each with a pair of many-jointed legs. Most crustaceans breathe with gills.

Growing larger is a problem inside a hard suit of armor, so crustaceans shed, or molt, their skeleton, and replace it with a new, larger one. When the old skeleton splits, the soft animal crawls out; the new skeleton, which has been forming under the old one, is pumped full of water and stretched to a larger size before it hardens.

Two pairs of antennae "sense" the surroundings. Some crustaceans use antennae for food-gathering or forming a breathing tube.

This crab uses its jointed pairs of legs for walking. Other crustaceans use legs for swimming, digging, food-gathering or even cradling their eggs.

The claw is used for defense and food-gathering.

Carapace

Echinoderms

Echinoderm (say "ek-eye-no-derm") means "spiny-skin," and these animals fit their name perfectly. They all have spines, a round body divided into five parts (often with five arms) and an internal skeleton. They don't have heads! Most echinoderms feed through a central mouth on the underside of the body, close to the sand, and breathe through their skin and tube feet. They also have tiny pincers covering the body. Echinoderms include sea stars, sea urchins and sand dollars.

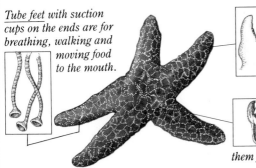

Tube feet with suction cups on the ends are for breathing, walking and moving food to the mouth.

The pincers are used as defense weapons, body cleaners and food grabbers.

The spines are for protection. Sea urchins and sand dollars also use them for digging and movement.

Look on a Sandy Beach

Sandy beaches often seem empty of life, but don't be deceived! Small holes in the wet sand probably mean there are clams buried below. A wandering trail through the sand might show that a moon snail has been searching for food. Animals here live beneath the surface or hide under seaweed to escape the sun, wind and constantly shifting sand. For you, the beach is a great place to walk barefoot, but for a beach creature it's the hardest place of all to live.

Mole Crab

APPEARANCE: The oval mole crab, or sandbug, is about as long as your little finger and doesn't look at all like the other crabs. Its legs are paddle-shaped at the tips. It has two pairs of antennae, covered with fine hairs, and two eyes attached to long stalks at the front of its body. The gray abdomen is bent underneath the body.

FOOD: Plankton and tiny bits of decaying plants and animals.

NOTES: As the waves wash back out to sea, the mole crab sticks up its feathery antennae and traps plankton on the fringes. The two smaller antennae, each divided into two parts, form a tube through which the animal breathes.

Mole Crab

BEACH PROJECT

Watch for mole crabs being carried to shore on the waves. If you don't see any, then walk toward the water and look for tiny bubbles shooting up from beneath the surf. This probably means that a mole crab is digging into the sand under the water. Quickly scoop there with your bucket lid. This little crustacean is fast, but see if you can be faster!

When you catch a mole crab, hold it carefully in your hand. Feel it try to dig into your palm. Add some water to your bucket and gently lay the crab inside. Watch how quickly the paddle-shaped legs move.

Now pick up the crab and dump the water out of your bucket. Add an inch or two of sand to the bottom, then some water. Put the crab in and watch how quickly it digs. Zip! It's gone. Did you notice that the animal dug backward into the sand?

Put the crab back in the surf. It will burrow in and start feeding as if nothing had happened.

Moon Jellyfish

APPEARANCE: The moon jellyfish is shiny white and has many short stinging tentacles hanging from the edge of its body. Just as the sea anemone paralyzes its prey with these cells, so does a jellyfish. Four arms hang down to help trap and move food into the mouth nearby. Out of water this animal looks like a blob of jelly, but at sea the jellyfish is a delicate, graceful creature that drifts with the currents.

FOOD: Small animals and plankton, captured by the tentacles.

NOTES: Moon jellyfish are cnidarians that move freely, swimming up and down by opening and closing their umbrellas. But they aren't strong enough to swim against the current, so they're carried far and wide by currents, winds and tides. Many are washed ashore during storms or rough seas. Often jellyfish from warmer waters are carried to our shores, and some are deadly. Watch out—even stranded ones can give a painful sting!

Moon Jellyfish

Moon Snail

Moon Snail

APPEARANCE: The moon snail is a univalve that can grow as large as a grapefruit! Its foot is huge, too, almost covering the shell as the snail plows through sand. When the snail pulls itself into its shell, a lot of water pours out to make room for the foot. The spiral shell is smooth and sand-colored. If you find the broken shell of a moon snail along the driftline, you may see the central column inside the spiral.

FOOD: Clams, mussels and even dead fish.

NOTES: This snail uses its radula to drill a large hole in a bivalve's shell to get to the animal inside. Sometimes it just smothers the clam with its giant foot! In the spring, the moon snail lays thousands of eggs, then glues them into a "collar" with mucus and sand. This sand collar sits around the snail's foot until the snail creeps forward and eventually leaves it behind. Rubbery sand collars can be found in the intertidal area, but don't pick them up—if they crumble, the eggs will dry out and die.

Softshell Clam

APPEARANCE: The softshell clam has a thin, brittle shell that is easily cracked. The shell is covered with a flaky brown skin at the edges and has very rough growth lines. Both ends of the shell remain slightly open.

FOOD: Plankton, filtered from the water.

A soft-shell cousin called the geoduck (say "goo-ee-duck") is all siphon and very little shell. If you go digging for a geoduck, you could end up in a hole deep enough to stand in!

The siphon.

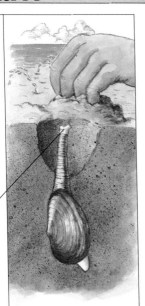

Softshell Clam

BEACH PROJECT

Walk toward the water at low tide. If you see water squirting out of small holes, you've probably found a bed of clams. This water is being pushed out as the clams pull their siphons into their shells.

Dig with your lid beside one of the holes. (Be careful—some clams are easily crushed.) Pile your diggings where there are no other siphon holes. Don't give up! The softshell clam and others have long siphons that enable them to live deep in the sand, so you may have to dig down past the length of your arm.

When you reach a clam, scoop the sand from around it. Then cup your hand around the clam and ease it out of its hole. Fill your bucket with water so that you can rinse off the shell.

Now put some sand in your bucket and place the clam on top. The mollusk may extend its foot to burrow into the sand as you watch.

When you've finished, fill in the hole that you dug. Return the clam to a shallow hole and cover it lightly with sand.

Beach Hopper

Beach Hopper

APPEARANCE: The busy beach hopper, also known as the sand flea, may be as small as your fingernail or as long as your little finger. The head has two pairs of antennae; on some beach hoppers, these antennae are bright orange. The body is divided into many segments, with seven pairs of walking legs. The abdomen, near the end of the body, has three pairs of flipped-up legs and curves in toward the animal's underside.

FOOD: Algae and decaying plant material.

MINI BEACH PROJECT

Look for beach hoppers under wet seaweed. When you uncover one, watch it lie on one side and flip itself forward by straightening out its abdomen. Cup your hand around a beach hopper, place it in your bucket and wait. Boing! The beach hopper jumps out and is gone!

Sand Dollar

Sand Dollar

APPEARANCE: Sand dollars are flat and round, like large coins, and covered with short, dark brown spines. On the top is a flower-like pattern of five petals. The tiny tube feet found in the petal pattern are used for breathing. On the underside are five grooves that lead to the mouth in the center. Tiny tube feet border here, too, but these feet are used for passing food along the grooves to the mouth.

FOOD: Plankton and tiny bits of plants that settle on top of the sand dollar. The food is moved by mucus on the skin to the outer edge of the body and then to the tube feet on the underside.

NOTES: Like sea stars and sea urchins, the sand dollar is an echinoderm. It uses its short spines like shovels to dig in at an angle, with the rear end sticking up. Live sand dollars can sometimes be found near the low-tide line. Look on the beach for their empty skeletons, bleached white by the sun.

Fiddler Crab

APPEARANCE: Fiddler crabs are small brown or dark gray crabs found by the hundreds on the Atlantic coast. The male has one small claw and one huge one that is a lighter color than the body; he waves his large "fiddle" claw to attract the attention of a female. The female's claws are both small, so she's easy to tell apart from the male.

FOOD: Bits of plants and animals found in mud and sand. The crab rolls the mud in front of its mouth and picks out the good bits.

Fiddler Crab

BEACH PROJECT

As the tide is going out, visit a marsh on the back side of the beach away from the surf. Look for small balls of mud beside holes in the surface to locate a fiddler crab's home or burrow.

Fiddler crabs are one of the many crustaceans that can change color! At night, they are light; during the day, they are dark. The tide times also affect their color: at high tide, when they are hidden in their burrows, they are light-colored; then, as they come out to search for food in the mud, they slowly darken.

Try to catch a fiddler. They move sideways like lightning, so you'll have to be very fast. First catch a female, then a male. Grasp the female from behind with your thumb under her body and your forefinger on her back. When you catch a male, use your free hand to hold the large claw so he can't grab you. But be careful—if the crab is determined to escape, you could be left holding a claw but no crab! (If this happens, the crab will slowly grow a new one.)

Collect Shells…

Shells are beautiful. You'll get an idea of the mollusk's many colors and patterns, shapes and sizes, as you search for their shells along the driftline. Often you'll pick up just half of the animal's shell; the other half may have been tossed up farther along the beach. The shells that you find are only "skeletons"; their owners have already died. Before taking a shell home, be sure it is *not* a living animal.

Besides the eight shells shown on these pages, there are many other kinds to search for and discover. If you want to know more about shells and the animals that made them, see *The Audubon Society Field Guide to Seashells*.

Cockle

● The COCKLE has a very short siphon, so it lives close to the surface of the sand—and sometimes on top! Its big, thick shell is heavily ridged and has a heart shape if you hold it sideways.

● The SAND CLAM (Pacific) vacuums up sand and water with its long separate siphons. The shell is elongated at the foot end, while the siphon end is rounded. Many small, shiny, brightly colored Tellin clams, found on both coasts, are shaped like this larger relative.

• The JINGLE SHELL CLAM attaches itself to rocks by a strong thread that reaches out through a hole in the bottom half of the shell. Look for a round, rough shell with a pearly inside. String a few together and hang them up as a wind chime.

• The RAZOR CLAM is a speed demon when it comes to digging into the sand! Be careful of this clam's shell—its edges are razor-sharp. Its shape is long and oval, and it has a shiny, brownish covering.

• The Atlantic QUAHOG was collected by coastal natives, who made the shells into wampum

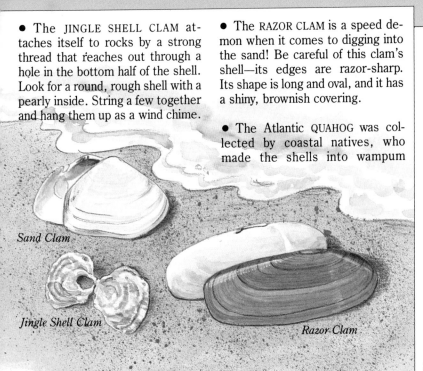

Sand Clam

Jingle Shell Clam

Razor Clam

...and More Shells

beads. Look for a thick, oval shell edged with splashes of purple.

• The Atlantic SURF CLAM is also big, but its siphon is small. After a storm, you may find hundreds of surf clams that have been plucked from their shallow burrows by the waves and thrown onto the beach. Look for a thick, triangular shell

covered in a light brown skin. Many smaller kinds of surf clams can be found on both coasts, too.

• The Pacific HORSE CLAM burrows very deep into the sand and its enormous, leathery siphon reaches far up to the surface. Its fat, heavy shell (larger than your

Quahog

Surf Clam

two hands put side by side!) has a flaky brown coating near the edges and a large opening at one end where the siphon once stuck out.

• The Pacific LITTLENECK CLAM, named for its small "neck," or siphon, burrows near the surface in sand and cobble. The shell is about the size of your palm, with a scalloped edge made by the ridges.

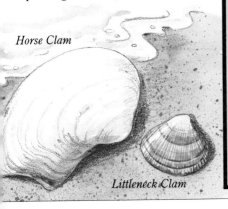

Horse Clam

Littleneck Clam

BEACH PROJECT

Look for shells that have a small, round hole in them. This is where a whelk or moon snail has drilled through the shell to get to the soft mollusk body inside.

Find the large, pearly, circular spots on the inside of a shell where the muscles were. The mantle was attached along the long line leading toward the edge. The line that sweeps back from the mantle line to the muscle mark shows where the siphon lay when not in use.

Pick up a snail shell and hold it with the point up and the opening facing you. If the opening is on your right, the snail is "right-handed"; if on the left, it's "left-handed."

39

Look in a Tidepool

A tidepool is a miniature sea world. Sit down and spend some time observing the life here: a sea star on the prowl; an anemone waiting for its lunch; crabs and fish peering out from around rocks. The return of the tide means a new supply of food, water and oxygen for these animals. Tidepool life is always a little easier and a lot busier just after high tide.

Sea Anemone

Sea Anemone

APPEARANCE: Sea anemones look like bright, beautiful flowers growing underwater. They can be as tiny as a dime or as large as a dinner plate.

FOOD: Small fish, crabs, worms, shrimp.

NOTES: These cnidarians are always hungry. Any small animal that touches the sea anemone's tentacles is paralyzed by the stinging cells. Then the anemone stuffs the animal into its mouth with its tentacles. Soon after, it spits out small, indigestible bits of its meal!

MINI BEACH PROJECT

Drop a small piece of meat onto a sea anemone's tentacles and see what happens!

Now gently nudge the anemone with a small stick. In go the tentacles, and the anemone protects itself by appearing to be a lifeless blob.

Chiton

Chiton

APPEARANCE: Chitons, or "sea cradles," have eight overlapping valves that allow them to roll up like armadillos when threatened. Around the edge of their shell is a girdle of tough flesh, which can be smooth or hairy. Some chitons are brightly colored; others are brown or gray, sometimes with a red or orange girdle. Most chitons are small, but one giant variety grows to the length of a loaf of bread!

FOOD: Algae and tiny animals scraped off rocks by a licking motion of the radula.

NOTES: The teeth on this mollusk's radula contain a lot of silicon and iron, which makes them hard. Scientists have discovered that the iron also makes the teeth magnetic! The chiton feeds at night; then, as dawn approaches, it creeps slowly along on its foot toward a dark place in the tidepool. Just like limpets, some chitons return to homesites, where they use their girdle and foot as a suction cup to clamp tightly onto the undersides of rocks.

Hermit Crab

APPEARANCE: The tiny hermit crab doesn't look at all like a crab. That's because this crustacean is usually found inside an empty periwinkle or whelk shell. The hermit hangs on to its "house" by means of special hooks on its rear legs. The front walking legs are dotted or banded with bright colors. Note that the right front claw is larger than the left. You can also see the very long antennae.

FOOD: Just about anything, including bits of dead plants and animals.

Hermit Crab

BEACH PROJECT

Find a fast-moving snail shell, and you've probably spotted a hermit crab. Wait for more crabs to appear, then watch them rush about the tidepool, dragging their houses with them and often fighting with each other over new houses. Some carry an anemone on their shell to ward off octopus attacks!

Gently pick up a crab, house and all. The crab will hide inside for a bit, but be patient—eventually it will come out and move around on the palm of your hand.

For a close-up look at the hermit (or any other creature), you can turn the bucket into a magnifier. Add some water to the bucket and place the crab inside. Now cover the opening with a piece of clear plastic wrap and hold it tightly in place with an elastic band. Scoop a small amount of water on top to make a small pool that hangs down slightly (not too far!) inside. Now look through the pool. Can you see the hermit's antennae?

Mussel

Mussel

APPEARANCE: Mussels usually grow in clusters and have thin, bluish shells, sometimes with traces of brown or white. The inside of the shell is pearly blue. Like the oyster, the mussel doesn't have a siphon; instead, it opens its valves to let in water.

FOOD: Plankton and decaying bits of plants and animals.

MINI BEACH PROJECT

Take a peek at the mussel's "beard," the network of little threads by which the animal secures itself to the rocks. Made by the mussel's foot, the threads harden in the seawater and stick like glue to the rock. They also house other small creatures—even small fish!

Sea Urchin

Sea Urchin

APPEARANCE: Sea urchins are covered with long, stiff spines of bright colors, often green, red or purple. They can grow to the size of a slightly flattened baseball.

FOOD: Algae and bits of dead animals.

NOTES: Sea urchins look as if they're walking on stilts—and some are! Some even use their spines to burrow into rock. Most, however, pull themselves along with their tube feet, using the spines for protection and digging. The five pairs of tube feet around the mouth are adapted for breathing.

MINI BEACH PROJECT

Watch how this echinoderm puts its spines to use. Gently nudge one with a small stick, and you'll see the spines move forward. Now touch it with a large piece of shell: away move the spines to expose the pincers, which contain a poison that drives off attackers and stuns smaller prey.

47

Sea Star

APPEARANCE: The common sea star can be as big as a dinner plate (or bigger!) and is bright purple, orange, yellow, red or brown. Five short, thick arms are attached to the large central body of this echinoderm, and at the tip of each is an eyespot that lets the animal see light and dark. Sea stars have an amazing ability to grow back arms that were lost to an enemy.

Sea Star

FOOD: Oysters, mussels, snails, limpets, crabs, barnacles and sea urchins.

BEACH PROJECT

Grasp a sea star around the central disk. If it holds on tightly to a rock, leave it alone; otherwise, you might pull out some of its tube feet with your tugging.

Touch the rough, spiny skin. Now turn the sea star over so that its back touches the hairs on your arm. Leave it there awhile, and then slowly move the animal away. You'll find that the animal's little body pincers have grabbed the hairs on your arm. Try this against the hair on your head, too!

Look at the tube feet. The suction cups on the ends are for "walking" and hanging on to food. The sea star pulls on a mollusk to open the shell, then turns its stomach inside out, pushes it into the mollusk and digests its meal right inside the shell!

Scrape some fine particles of old shells onto the back of a sea star and watch its pincers crush the particles into powder. Then mucus and little hairs on the skin move the dust off the animal's back.

Remember to return the sea star to the tidepool.

Fish in a Tidepool

Many small fish are found in tidepools. Some, such as flounders, are the young of fish that live in deep water; when the tide goes out, they remain in the pool. Most of these fish are well adapted for tidepool life. They are small, usually no longer than your hand, with flattened or tapered bodies. Some have special ways of clinging to rocks or climbing over them. Colors on their body slowly change to match their environment. Look for them nestled in the sand or hiding in dark crevices or under rocks; try to shoo one into your bucket for a close look. When the high tide returns, they swim out to search for food in the shallows.

• A CLINGFISH sticks itself to rocks, seaweed or shells with fins that make a suction cup under its body. From above, this fish looks like a large tadpole. If you look closely, you'll see that it has no scales!

• A GUNNEL looks more like a small, colorful eel. It hides under rocks and seaweed, and if disturbed it will slither away like a snake to another hiding place.

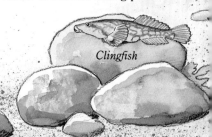

Clingfish

• A SCULPIN has sharp spines on its head and often on its back. One variety has a home tidepool and can find its way back there from long distances. Another uses its large side fins to walk over rocks. And one remarkable sculpin actually rests out of water on top of the rocks!

• A FLOUNDER nestles its flat body into the sand and almost seems to disappear. Small flounders may be trapped in tidepools, but you can see them as the tide moves over the sand, too. Look at the flounder's eyes—both of them are on the same side of its body! As the fish was growing, one eye moved over the top of its head.

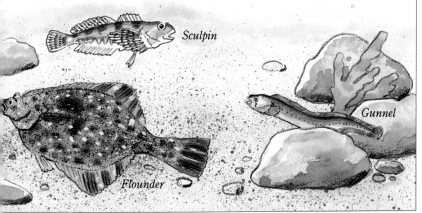

Sculpin

Gunnel

Flounder

Look on a Rocky Beach

There's lots of life on a rocky beach! Plants and animals can find many places to hold on to here, as well as many places to hide from the wind and sun and pounding waves. High up on the beach, periwinkles cling tightly during low tide, sealed in their own little houses. Next come masses of barnacles, cemented in place. Rockweed and mussels layer the rocks, and small creatures find shelter under them. Crabs hide under stones or scuttle across the cobbles.

Limpet

Limpet

APPEARANCE: The limpet is a mollusk that looks like a lopsided pointed hat. The edges of its shell can be smooth or wavy.

FOOD: Algae scraped off rocks by the radula.

NOTES: During the day, limpets cling to rocks close to the algae. Some even have a "home"—a groove worn into a rock in a circular shape that fits their shell perfectly and keeps them from drying out at low tide. If you see such a groove, you've probably found an old homesite.

MINI BEACH PROJECT

To withdraw all the way into its shell, the limpet has to make room by pushing out much of the water held in the shell and body. Touch a limpet with your finger. Water will suddenly ooze out as the animal pulls in its body and clamps down tightly with its suction-cup foot.

Periwinkle

Periwinkle

APPEARANCE: A periwinkle is a chubby little snail. Its spiraled shell is usually brown, gray or black, sometimes with speckles or bands of lighter colors. The big spiral at the base of the shell is where the body lies. The topmost spiral is the oldest part of the shell.

FOOD: Algae and decaying plant material, scraped off rocks with the radula. As the tiny teeth on the radula wear down, sharp new teeth are pushed forward to replace them.

NOTES: Some periwinkles approach the sea only to wet their gills for breathing. The periwinkle creeps along on its strong foot, moving first to one side, then to the other; put one in your bucket, and you may see it skate up the side. Sometimes you'll find hundreds upon hundreds of these small univalves making their way over rocks, shells and seaweed.

Acorn Barnacle

APPEARANCE: Acorn barnacles are crustaceans. At low tide, they look like small volcanoes sitting on rocks and shells. Six hard plates protect the soft body inside, and the top is closed tightly by four more plates. Masses of barnacles attach themselves to rocks and other solid surfaces—including the bodies of whales!

Adult Barnacle

FOOD: Plankton.

NOTES: Barnacle larvae swim freely in the sea until it's time to settle down. Often picking a spot where traces of whitish "cement" have been left behind by another barnacle, the larva stands on its head and cements itself in place. After changing to the adult form, it builds permanent walls around its body.

BEACH PROJECT

Look for a cluster of adult barnacles. Tap gently on the hard outer coverings. The barnacle never molts its volcano shell. It does, however, molt a layer of hard skin that covers the soft body inside. As the body grows, more shell and cement are added, always to the bottom of the walls. Thus these crustaceans grow slowly outward and upward. If you could build the top of a sandcastle first and then add to it from the bottom, you'd be building the way a barnacle does!

Scoop some clear seawater into your bucket and gently place the rock, barnacle side up, on the bottom. Set the bucket in a cool, sheltered spot and wait patiently. You may be able to watch the barnacle feed itself. First the top of its shell opens up. Then out come six pairs of feathery legs called cirri. Watch the legs scoop down, combing plankton from the water, until finally they move the food to the mouth inside the walls.

Remember to return the rock to the beach, barnacle side up.

Whelk

Whelk

APPEARANCE: The whelk, also known as the dogwinkle, is a large snail about half the length of a new crayon. The shell has ridges that follow the spirals around the shell. In quiet waters, the ridges are ruffled and intricate; on beaches with strong waves, the shell is smooth! Whelks are usually brown, gray or white, sometimes with darker bands. Some may be pale orange or yellow.

FOOD: Barnacles, mussels, oysters and clams.

NOTES: The whelk, a small relative of the conch, lays little, oat-shaped, pale yellow eggs in clusters on the underside of rocks; when the eggs hatch, miniature, fully formed snails emerge. This mollusk is a meat-eater and feeds by drilling a small hole with its radula into the shell of its prey. Then it licks and sucks out the soft body inside. It can take a whelk more than three days to drill and eat an oyster!

Oyster

Oyster

APPEARANCE: Oysters are bivalves whose pearly shells can be either white or gray and are sometimes splashed with purple. They attach themselves to rocks by only one valve, which often remains in place after the oyster has died. Perhaps you'll find a rock with a valve still attached to it. The shape of the shell will match the shape of the rock that the oyster is cemented to, but the two rough valves never match each other—the top valve is smaller and flatter than the attached bottom one. If you find a hand-size oyster, it has probably been growing there for three or four years.

FOOD: Plankton and tiny parts of plants and animals, filtered by the gills.

NOTES: Unlike other bivalves, oysters have neither a foot nor a siphon. They feed only when the tide covers them; opening their valves, they let the water flow between them and over the gills, which remove oxygen and food.

Shore Crab

APPEARANCE: The shore crab, found on the Pacific coast, is a small crustacean—only about the size of a quarter! Like all other crabs, it has 10 legs; the first pair of legs are larger and are called claws, or pincers. This crab may be purplish-brown with purple spots on its claws. A similar variety is greenish without spots but with hairy legs.

FOOD: Almost anything, including dead or decaying food as well as seaweeds, especially sea lettuce. Crabs are important as scavengers; they help keep the beach clean.

Shore Crab

BEACH PROJECT

Find a shore crab hiding under a rock or seaweed. The crab may sit up on its walking legs and try to scare you with its claws, but most likely it will scurry away sideways. Most crabs are expert crawlers, but they can't swim.

Pick up the crab carefully and place it in your bucket. (Most crabs can give a sharp pinch, but shore crabs are usually too small to hurt you.) Gently tap the back of the crab. What you feel is the hard, protective carapace. See if you can spot the eyes on the front edge.

To find out if the crab is a male or female, pick it up from the hind end with your thumb under the body and your forefinger on top, and then look underneath. The little shape under your thumb is the abdomen. If the abdomen is long and thin, the crab is a male; if it is round and wide, you've found a female. You may see clusters of tiny eggs poking out from under the female's abdomen. Always be extra gentle with a mother crab.

Return the crab to the area where you found it.

Beach Birds

Look for these three common birds on your beach.

• The GREAT BLUE HERON is as tall as you are! If you see a heron standing still in shallow water, it could be hunting. You may see the heron grab a fish, turn it around and swallow it head first.

• The SANDERLING is one of the many small sandpipers that scurry along the receding waves, searching for food. In summer, its feathers are rust-colored; in winter, they are very light gray. This coloring helps the bird blend into the beach.

• The HERRING GULL has a red spot on the gull's lower bill. During nesting season, the chicks know to

Herring Gull

Sanderling

peck at this spot when they want to be fed. The pecking makes the parent bring up the half-digested food it has carried back to the nest.

Great Blue Heron

BEACH PROJECT

Watch the gulls and crows flying overhead. Some of them may be carrying snails or clams. See if they drop the shells onto the rocks below. Often the same shell has to be dropped many times before it cracks open and the bird can feed on the body inside.

Find a feather and look at it closely. Each side of the hollow center shaft has many rows of tiny hooks that fasten together like the teeth of a zipper. When birds preen themselves with their beaks, they are in effect doing up their zippers. Try preening yourself! Pull apart a row of feather hooks, then run your fingers up the hooks a few times to interlock them again. (Remember, a bird has had more practice than you!)

Beach Names

Common Name	Scientific Name(s)
Acorn barnacle *p. 56*	*Balanus balanoides* (A) *Balanus glandula (P)
Beach hopper *p. 32*	*Orchestia platensis* (A) **Orchestia traskiana* (P)
Chiton *p. 43*	*Chaetopleura apiculata* (A) **Tonicella lineata* (P)
Fiddler crab *p. 34*	*Uca pugilator* (A)
Hermit crab *p. 44*	*Pagurus acadianus* (A) **Pagurus granosimanus* (P)
Limpet *p. 54*	**Notoacmea testudinalis* (A) *Collisella pelta* (P)
Mole crab *p. 26*	*Emerita talpoida* (A) *Emerita analoga (P)
Moon jellyfish *p. 28*	*Aurelia aurita*

*Not illustrated in this book.

A = Atlantic coast; P = Pacific coast

Common Name	Scientific Name(s)
Moon snail *p. 29*	**Polinices duplicatus* (A) *Polinices lewisii* (P)
Mussel *p. 46*	*Mytilus edulis*
Oyster *p. 59*	*Crassostrea virginica* (A) **Crassostrea gigas* (P)
Periwinkle *p. 55*	*Littorina littorea* (A) **Littorina scutulata* (P)
Sand dollar *p. 33*	**Echinarachnius parma* (A) *Dendraster excentricus* (P)
Sea anemone *p. 42*	*Metridium senile (A) *Anthopleura xanthogrammica* (P)
Sea star *p. 48*	*Asterias forbesi (A) *Pisaster ochraceus* (P)
Sea urchin *p. 47*	*Strongylocentrotus droebachiensis*
Shore crab *p. 60*	*Hemigrapsus nudus* (P)
Softshell clam *p. 30*	*Mya arenaria*
Whelk *p. 58*	*Nucella lapillus (A) *Nucella lamellosa* (P)